Bloodstream

Praise for *Bloodstream*

Sarah Carey's second collection opens the vein of her life to take inventory of what is given, what is lost, and what is shared. "My words, my tongue, my tone, are never mine alone," her speaker tells us. In *Bloodstream* the poems move "through history handed down," and gaze unflinchingly at family tragedies and with eyes of love on all that remains—the dogs, the sisters, the beloved, the water and trees of Florida, to find "that heart beside my own bud heart, / from which all new leaves come."

—Lisa Zimmerman, author of *The Light at the Edge of Everything* and *Sainted*

Blood and wonder run through Sarah Carey's tender, self-effacing second volume of poetry where loss plays its upper hand with love in a discourse that begins with the query: Who were we when others couldn't see? The question propels us through incidentals of existence: aging, the demise of parents, and one's own procession through the poles of being. There's a strange and fortuitous literary underpinning of science in this voice, enlivening, and deepening eloquent language of the author's self-given task: how to discern nature vs. nurture comprising her journey—to the yet unlocated land of oneself.

—Sean Sexton, author of *Portals* and *May Darkness Restore*

With a keen lyric longing and a voice that blends tenderness and candor, the poems of Sarah Carey's *Bloodstream* ponder lineage, the *who* and *how* of one woman's becoming. These poems roam the complex embodied experiences of touching a healing horse, trying on a dead mother's bodysuit to find it does not fit, and entering the breath "that knows just how far back, how deep to go." They explore perception in the context of aging, memory, discovery and desire, love and grief. Carey's work asks what it means to witness the world through the life and lens of a woman artist, revealing tensions between creator and creation, seen and unseen, telling and untold, the "artist overlooking the Maine meadow" and "the woman overlooked." Self-portraits invoke the speaker as a longleaf pine who will "draw breath from toes to gut, lungs to throat, all the way up," and as a royal palm whose "roots…reach deep enough to threaten a foundation." There is a claiming here, and a reckoning—a celebration of endurance in an intimate, open-eyed remembering.

—Sally Rosen Kindred, author of *Where the Wolf*

Bloodstream

Poems

Sarah Carey

MERCER UNIVERSITY PRESS
Macon, Georgia

MUP/ P736

Published by Mercer University Press
1501 Mercer University Drive
Macon, Georgia 31207

30 29 28 27 26 5 4 3 2 1

Books published by Mercer University Press are printed on acid-free paper that meets the requirements of the American National Standard for Information Sciences—Permanence of Paper for Printed Library Materials.

Printed and bound in the United States.

This book is set in Adobe Garamond.

Cover/jacket design by Burt&Burt.

ISBN 979-8-89736-013-0
Cataloging-in-Publication Data is available from the Library of Congress

Contents

I Revisit What Comes to Me

I dedicate this book to the memories of those who gave me life and those who gave them life—my parents, grandparents, and the countless ancestors whose legacy I carry—along with those of cherished animal companions who have walked beside me and others I have loved. And to William Woolfitt, a tireless advocate of poets and poetry, whose editorial guidance and encouragement made this book possible.

“But so with all, from babes that play
At hide-and-seek to God afar,
So all who hide too well away
Must speak and tell us where they are.”

—Robert Frost

MERCER UNIVERSITY

MERCER UNIVERSITY PRESS

Endowed by

TOM WATSON BROWN

and

THE WATSON-BROWN FOUNDATION, INC.

Who We Were When Others Couldn't See Us

Anchorage

If an anchorage is a holdfast,
is root-like, fixes aquatic organisms
to their substrate—

think kelp, or how a spider's silken tethers
help it move—

perhaps a bloodstream is an anchorage,
scaffold, a branching out
from origin to vein, lineage

to story, a riverbed. I flow up
to meet you, protean
hypothesis. Dwell in echo,

undertow. Where we come from
doesn't ordain what we cling to.

Ars Poetica: Negative Capability

After the life model rises to dress
and another class vanishes into the night,

the last artist returns her charcoal
to the absence of light,

leafs through leftover sketches
her fingers pressed to life.

Among the outlines, silhouettes,
she divines an ancestor—

a smudged remembrance, imprint—
sees her face in the blur

between now and then, in the lack
of color. Keats's chameleon.

In the studio, a galaxy of newsprint
hides its black holes, holds

the deepening dark. Stars etched on a sky canvas
mirror evolutionary experiments.

But wasn't the point a universe reversed?
White space or invisible history?

Who we were when others couldn't see?

Friesian Story

But we can't say *beautiful*, I learned
in approvals. Rather, describe the Friesian mane,

its tail, as long and thick, its legs
by their trademark feathers

some adjectives still being acceptable
though Mark Twain said when you catch one,

kill it, along with your extraneous color and verbs.

I grasp at words my editors will keep
for the ebony body, a build better than statuesque,

for this warmblood—a noun,
in this instance, *warm* is allowed—

though Friesian, as proper, is capped
and anyone knowing the breed doesn't need

my apt description of how the stallion survived
its particular gastric impaction, commonly known

as colic, or the scope of the J-incision
the surgeon sliced down its side, the number of stitches

or a background of 2,000 years of history,
even the breed's near extinction,

but that's a long story, if you want one
of hope, if we're allowed to call it that—

a comeback, for today. Rather say elegance
without saying it, say all-black

is the standard adhered to by most registries,
that only a single white star on the forehead

is possible for a purebred,
but what I really want to tell you

is after its weeklong recovery from surgery
I touched this horse of many hands

with my own, then put them to work
I could still do, to share this draft

horse with you, leave you wanting,
let the lack of language speak.

What did Frost say?
Nothing gold can stay.

Globus

I wake hungry, restless, stuck—
something I can't swallow. *Forgive me*
wanting more than a god

can give, I pray. I want to believe
divinity lives—within my body,
out of my hands. Years ago, I passed

the peace of the Lord in a pew.
Now, I toss, I want
my peace back. I reckon with the arbiter

who shuffles order, the shark who deals
luck like cards. I turn,
I tuck my head, take from childlessness

a holy solitude, a shell. Call me
mollusk, crustacean, reptile-
in-exile. Imagine Marvell's drop of dew—

so self-contained! But I know better,
I know burrows, dreams beyond
the terminus of my ancestral thread.

Consistency

Like bacteria that thrive
in moist, warm environments—
behind my ears, under my neck—

migrated to oases: men to quench
my endless thirst, bodies like oceans
to absorb me. I'd swim

against their current. Even now, on shore,
I'll wake with parched lips.

***

Want hits a roof and shreds
its shingles, a garment
worn to the bone.

Threadbare, I'd learn
what I loved most was fluid,
porous, perfectly healthy.

***

Let's go for fro-yo, I say
to my husband on this day like any other
in hot, humid Florida.

***

The purplest passion flower fades

in fields where we no longer go,
near rivers that no longer flow.

When chocolate and vanilla soft-serve swirls
to settle ice-cold, smooth, content
within its dish, I know why

my taste bud cells crave soothing
sweetness, live cultures—good for us—
spoon to mouth consistency dispensed.

Delivery

It's just a box, Mother says
as we drive north from Tallahassee to the service.
Grandmother S. is an angel now,

hair unpermed, in the simplest of gowns.
Above us as cargo she flies
to the middle of the family plot

where beneath a maroon canopy
and North Carolina's turning black gum, sugar maple,
steel sky, on the coldest day of fall,

last branches of family weave
a tight circle, heads bowed beneath funeral sprays—
blue iris, white mum, baby's breath.

Later, I'll cart the dying heartleaf philodendron
from Grandmother S.'s porch
to my car, to my stoop,

snip healthy stems above the nodes,
then drop the leafless ends in water,
attempt to tempt the tendrils to root.

Bearings

(Oct. 13, 2023)

All day we drove the parkway,
listened for bugling elk
but heard only the roar of exhaust,

the howl of bearings, close to Clingman's Dome
in the highest of seasons, everyone hot
to hike, until we finally gave up

on waiting, squealed our wheels in a tight
turnaround, then headed to our rental cabin
home on loan.

***

Here and there, between angelica, aster,
my childhood stretches
from peaks to foothills

to flat Florida and back. I tell you tales my father told
to make our trips go faster,
point to lookouts we languished in,

stunned at the hills' stark relief.
How something stuck on the forest underside
remains unbearable.

***

Home on my father's 92nd birthday is a moving
forward, flashback, a yearning
for flocks of wild turkey, gangs of elk,

harbingers of luck. We crack
our windows, breathe in campfire smoke, a whiff
of cedar, fir. Deracinated, we orient.

A few more years may lie ahead, or not.

***

Long before elk were reintroduced
into Cataloochee, before the love would die,
my parents honeymooned here, or nearby

but all from the wedding party
are long gone. I imagine them quieting
in their abditive spaces,

wherever in the valley they lay down.

Discovery

When the faces I must put on
melt into one enemy.

When long shadows in my closet
mock my favorite sets and separates.

When my minimizing
pencil skirts no longer flatter.

When wrinkles blur the lines
of my sleek Irish linen suits.

When nothing I knew about myself
as true will fit, and in darkness I change.

When no statement scarf or patterned jacket
recollects the way I felt in old

merino layers, pilled cashmere,
in comfort clothes, and spring's silk shifts

aren't cool enough to calm my aging chill,
I stand at the mirror, planted

in tossed hangers, will myself whole.
I'll go to any lengths.

Watch me.

In the Men's Department at Montgomery Ward
(1980)

What size are you, what size are you?
You've outgrown the twelves,
caught somewhere between
the fourteen-sixteens, at that age
when a men's small no longer
hangs off your shoulders. I remember you
last year, your mother restless
outside of the dressing room.
I'd just clocked in, and I fitted you then.
You left without anything altered.
Now you're back for new armor,
anything to hide those raw insides from view,
disappear in aisles full of young men,
and I say you can win in this two-in-one NFL
zip-off sleeve jacket—shiny black
polyester-filled chintz, one size up,
cut loose, or skim the rack
for the last hooded, all-cotton FBI short coat
in red, white, and blue, not as thick,
does the trick nonetheless, thin protection
for your lean shoulders—
imagine the softness within, a light cape
fit for a prince.

All Max Couldn't Tell Me of Desire

Max ate two cups of food before
the phone rang, then begged for release
and I gave it—took a long phone call
as he dashed through the door, our yard
with no fence, many woods, a lake, snakes.
I talked longer than usual.
I was used to Max disappearing,
not to the chill I felt like a front
or a viral invasion. Red in the sky
pooled low near the lake, like a bleed.
As sun set and dark fell into each cavity
he'd dug in the dirt, I traced
each path he'd pranced, scanned sand
with my flashlight for prints. Ears pricked
for howl or splash, I stared at stars—
Where might Canis Major, Sirius lead?
I imagine him staring past my face
at deer near the water's edge, or at wild turkey foraging
near the old canoe. What could I have taken
as clue? Suddenly a keening, both tuning fork
and magnet, propelled me down our graded road
as my brights swept each ditch
until a still, dark shape appeared.
No stars blinked in the blank sky the moon left
when I pulled off on a stretch of shoulder,
pitched my body over his limp body, too late.

What I Tell My Unborn Children When They Ask Where We Come From

My words, my tongue, my tone,
are never mine alone. My endless strands
of DNA bespeak other passages:
maiden voyage of a train full of emigrants
to a promised land, or great-aunt Inez,
wife of Lorenzo, young rail hand,
switch tender, who fell to the track,
crushed under an engine in Fort Wayne
while cars were coupling. Later she left
and never came back. Eventually,
I saw my true conveyance: how migrations
swept me here from Ireland, England,
Germany, onto farms I worked until
the Western Carolina soil wore out,
then into mines and textile mills, the lumber
industry. How the South renewed
my blood. How despite my hardy stock,
I could never settle, moved from relative

to relative to matter in your most
nostalgic recollection, intuition's spark:
mass of muscle memory, fantasy mother.
I would speak of fullness manifested,
never barren but content, when asked
about regret. Some say what they might
do differently, if they could turn back time,
but let me set the record straight:
part of me broke in Roanoke, where

great-uncle Marshall, son of Daisy,
fell from a hotel window—*suicide*,
my mother said, though the death
certificate read *accident*. I imagine
shaking hands with Hugh, who married
Marshall's widow, Mary, gave her
grandson a namesake. This was fate,
I tell you, this was tenderness
I can't swear you'll inherit.

One Day's Inventory

One Day's Inventory

Flipped open my laptop to a home screen
fed with news: A bigger picture, breaking.

A record set for preventable deaths. Sat back
with black coffee, fake sugar. Sipped.

Later, I married the mop to the microfiber pad.
Doused the head with the best solution,

polished the wood floors, worn by now
so close to the tongue and groove.

Made a list. Checked a box or two.
Sprayed, then buffed the mirror dry.

Stared down everything my walls encased, at all
I'd left undone, and faced the face

of my undoing. When the rain slowed,
I walked the dog.

An Origin Story

In the cabin where I was conceived,
where my great-uncle let us stay,

Mother organized belongings
for our move, while Father, straight
out of seminary, ministered,

as was his want, at a school
with mandatory chapel and vespers.

Where righteousness could be
compartmentalized, though I always believed
I came from some imagined justice.

In this tiny Southern town
where it was wise to not be too theological

or over-speak, Father spoke for the students
during the protests, sit-ins beginning
in bigger cities not far up the road.

In the era of Jim Crow.
Inside Mother's belly, where her blood

pumped parallel to mine, feeding my veins,
my heart in intervillous chambers,
I drew a way of knowing

from her body about the world that was
and yet was yet to be.

Eyes of Girls

On a shelf across from express lanes,
carts full of bargains and day-old bread,

a dozen dolls stare ahead in costumes
of kimono, dirndl, folk dress. In the aisles,

bent workers ablate debris
from a thousand susurrating footsteps.

Aproned women offer sweet samples for free.
I take every hand-out that appeals

to me: iced cinnamon-roll triangles, squares
of lemon cake as I watch the deep

and darting eyes of girls fixate on the display—
girls in crop tops, hair upswept in crescent clips,

cargo pants, crossbodies in full sway.
Once, in a time I barely remember,

dolls were for play. Later, lost or collected,
shelved, admired, as in this market

for all to see. Behind glass,
my mother's vintage dolls peer out at me—

corn husk, broom straw, cloth-bodied,
bowed and ribboned, tiny and tall

in shapes I absorbed, along with the knowing
she once held them close, at a time

when in her eyes, I imagine the world.

The Rose Bush

It wasn't so much I wanted to hurt
so much as I wanted to fight
the mite-spread virus
killing off my last stand of intentional

landscape—rose, rosette—
so one day after too many
like this, anger second-guessed,
I tackled the overgrown bush

arched over my driveway—
its build-up of a little dead each year
entangled with the little living—
wiped blood from my ungloved hands

my skin in the game, as if to resurrect
resistance. Left my whittled witness.

Heel of a Loaf

Grandmother S. favored the heel,
Mother said when I asked
about her mother's taste

as she passed peeled navel oranges,
soft-scrambled eggs. Now she's gluten-free,
so Mother's twice-proven loaves
are as long-gone as our ancestors

yet rise in memory. As children,
we fasted in Father's absence,
each homecoming a feast.

We held out for hot fudge sundaes—
Don't fill up on bread, he said,
left chocolate kisses under our pillows.

These days, we stay preoccupied
with our long valediction: a growing cyst,
a deafened ear, or fading eye
a doctor should have seen.

Grandmother S. left Mother the lazy Susan,
around which we spin the calendar,
circle appointments, phone numbers of friends

like a wheel of bad fortune.
Mother's skin grows thinner.
Mine and Sister's thickens
like a crust.

The Body Inside My Body

(1980)

Car salesmen speckle showroom floors,
drift periodically away for a drag

resurface, reeking of smoke
when they remember me circling,
say to holler if I need them, let me go

outside where I lose myself
in rows of color-coded mirrors

designating levels of trim. Men in polos
hawk best terms: low down, no interest
for the package with moonroof, premium

stereo. A door opens, I slide
into a seat with no memory, adjust.
Someone pushes my buttons

says I'm made for power everything—
steering, windows, locks, but I'm not automatic,
tire of test drives, turn

and toss their keys. They panic,
offer the last ditch take or leave. I take

my time. Once I burned through a wildfire haze
until I couldn't see, pulled over
when a wind gust opened the highway

shoulder. Breathed exhaust. Later, I learned
the gasket blew. There was no quick re-do.

From then on, I ran my rides into the ground,
like the body inside my body: revved, hot.
Dreamt older models, sleek sedans,

like Cutlass, Skylark,
pure, stripped down.

Orienteering

(Summer, 1994)

Heading north toward Ogunquit
10 miles from Newburyport
beaches flicker into view

—if you can call them beaches, I say,
Florida-spoiled. My midwestern father,
a transplant, reiterates what I grew up hearing:

how most people in our country
would gladly donate any innate sense —
eyeteeth, ear engram, (cuspid,

Latin word for point),
a conch's sound held in the nerve—
to live in our state, and then, entitled,

I couldn't comprehend what I took for granted—
a stable homeland, freedom to forecast
desire's itinerary. I seek

and scan. A broadcast warns
of thunderstorms on the horizon
and sure enough, static develops

in the console between us
in that rental sedan far from Boston:
the world ahead, maps in our laps

with their legends, my penned dots and stars,
we lean out our windows—instruments of wind—
in the worst heat wave

to hit New England in nearly 60 years,
we drive through history handed down—

shipbuilding's glory days, the advent of abolition,
a trio of churches still standing.
My father assures we'll get there yet,

his voice imprinted like Panhandle sand,
each shell I lifted, held.

The Land, the Sea, the Air

Some things I took for granted vanished
long ago: a store, a mall, a whole shopping plaza,

an entire country I grew up in, moving
state to state, when welcome signs

marked the borders, and no one spoke
of red and blue intent, or waves to change

the nation's constitution. Remember when
we were blank slates?

How did I outgrow my openness,
my eagerness to face the challenges I met?

We've survived shrinking human concern
for endangered species, carcinogens

in pesticides, too much ultraviolet,
but can't admit our threatened habitat—

exist instead in separate fantasies
of what life used to be, mailboxes that opened

and closed like gates to an abandoned land,
once brimming with cards of sympathy,

congratulations, and friends' confessions.
In the internet's wake, a vanishing.

I'd be lying if I said I don't dream
our mail carrier delivers ghostly

envelopes to my cul-de-sac
across decades, vast unpolluted seas—

my father's aerograms, his world flown
back to me, featherlight and blue as air.

For an Artist Painting Loss

En plein air, you use blue
as acute accent, for your mother's distant trees,
to inflect sky, or deepen nearby grass—
perhaps a shade like phthalocyanine—

light-fast, resistant to acids
and alkalis. Between brush strokes, you weigh
how memory filters truth.

**

A dream pigment, if fake, dancing
with copper atoms, phthalo—
say it like Thalo, a name fit for gods—

displaced Prussian blue in the 20th century
as the painters embraced a color unafraid to speak.

What's done in love is done well,
said van Gogh, a Prussian blue fan
in his day. Borne of cattle blood,
Prussian was blue accident—

consider "Starry Night," to which he added
cobalt and ultramarine.

Ask yourself which animal speaks to you
most boldly of its shape
and brush its insides out.

**

Even the least pressing of questions,
burgherish or peasantish, cannot survive
beneath this most azure of skies,
Szymborska wrote in that poem
about the medieval miniature.

Remember your mother in late-stage disease
stumbling on blue questions in the color task.
Catalyst of argument, rich queen,
phthalo croons from her palette:

push me, parcel out my views
in darker values, sweet spots, stain.

Here at the canvas, in the conveyance,
in the dying light, you train.

Self Portrait as Longleaf Pine

Not uprooted, not hunger-drawn,
never transplanted from my homeland,
I thrive within my North Florida confines,

much as a longleaf pine's armored core
protects from fire and stores blood sap,

whose taproot mass drops anchor
beneath a needled overstory—
told by my family so many times

I've memorized ancestors war-displaced,
storm-scattered, migrating from their shores to mine.
Smells carried on trade winds—

fruitcake, from my German side,
beef and potatoes from my Irish—

yet memory fades, while time, a careful surgeon,
debrides dead tissue from bole wounds
forming a callus, allowing new growth

but hoped-for seedlings don't arrive.
Meanwhile, the pine's resin weeps. My center holds
its xylem and its phloem.

I bank on spring
and the next and the next,

channel my ancestors' endurance.
In the thinned old forest,
I draw breath from toes

to gut, lungs to throat, all the way up,
claiming my brief space on earth,
like any native of this world.

Another Day's Inventory

Another Day's Inventory

When the rain slowed, I walked the dog
from whom I wrested one bottlecap, one shoe.

Clicked on a link to a network of bail funds,
found my country, my state. Hovered.

Faced quarantine roots in the mirror
bleeding into grey, then saw them fade

to ends, though split, still bright.
Remembered those halcyon days.

Stared at everything my walls encased.
Everything for so long, tirelessly, I'd polished.

Considered my money, my voice.
Spoke too soon, too often,

not at all, or far too late.

Wyeth's Women

seldom greet us face to face.
Take Helga, at the black canyon,
blonde braid falling behind.

He gives her back to us.

The museum docent approaches
the Lady of the House, who is opening
or closing the door,

we'll never know which, or why,
when we try to enter the painting,
nor who Christina was

that bleak day in the open field
when Wyeth spotted her, crawling—
as she would, the guide tells our tour group,

how she hated her wheelchair, crawled
everywhere, desperate or determined

not to be seen as weak, or not to be seen
at all, and inspired by either
her courage or her freakishness

Wyeth had his wife model her torso.

I imagine the light as it would have been
from the farmhouse, window admitting
that gold-flecked scrim. The artist

overlooking a Maine meadow,
the woman overlooked.

Making Soda Focaccia the Day of the Muslim Ban

We make dimples for olive oil,
little wells in the rolled dough

press edges to the sides of Swiss roll tins
then place our Kalamatas, rosemary sprigs
inside red-onion crescents:

quarter moon trifectas   shaved/pitted/torn
from Greek and Mediterranean roots

to be arranged four down and three across—
each square, various and varied.

So cosmopolitan are we in our class
near the sea at Ballycotton

where we've learned that Irish cooking
is anything but, as well as how to cut an onion
keeping the tip of the knife put

and how the key to perfect soda bread
is a light touch. The news sifts in:
an immigration order, Muslim ban.

We nudge stranded slices back to sanctuary,
memorize the steps: sieve/make a well

pour/make a claw   mix/ pull the hand
push/press/impress   upon us all

a route to sustenance: we scatter salt
we drizzle   rack our pans.

Let the high heat rise.

Grandmother's Will

(for Mother)

Forget the time it took, day in
day out, to warm supper,
schedule the help.

When you signed her checks for her,
I saw how time steals legibility,
how Grandmother S. lost the will or hid it,
kept us guessing until the end

when her fingers couldn't hold a pen
or her head, an account. I saw
a purple flecked topography of veins

in the slim legs you inherited
and I did not. How transparent,
my desire to stay young—
in body, in mind—adept.

When it comes to my mouth
I'm a grinder, says my dentist.
You could say what needed to be said

and sleep at night, but I dream of freeing
whatever is stuck on the roof
and flying, of Grandmother S.—

how she'd call us *dahlin,* with the long *ahh*
of Southern r-lessness, but nothing followed,
leaving us to guess why her endearments

trailed like ellipses, her short-lived smiles
for company, leaving us to wonder
if we read her tight lips right or not at all.

Recovery Is a Work in Progress, an Exoskeleton

I brought Max home in a box, tiny pup,
from a breeder soon after
the Gainesville student murders in 1990.

My fears disappeared,
my sleep returned, like the wrens
who abandoned my feeder

when we changed the suet
then came back and chirped away
as if nothing had happened.

Max ate everything: his proper food,
our cheese, dirt, wood,
the legs of my poplar cabinet

we puttied to save. To this day
the thought of him makes me weak.
No children for me all those years,

only his kiss. What would he want?
Steak fat, ginger snaps.
The last piece of cheesecake.

When I feel the world has no sweetness left,
or shudder at dark news,
I remember he redefined off-white,

lifting his chocolate lab fur from the couch
with strips of duct tape.
When I pull his collar from storage,

breathe it in, it reeks of must,
but I can't throw it out,
its cracked leather so like a second skin.

A Rare Disease

In the study, we work backwards:
who did what to whom, who took which drug
for pain? We chart methods of birth control
from pills to foam, to finally, withdrawal.
Cross the what-ifs off our lists.
Who else might we have exposed?
Who yet might learn from our mistakes?

We share which lines in our respective genes
could predispose us to this end,
exercise our possibilities, not excited,
not content, not with the long view of regret
but rather with the fixed eyes of predators
biding our time, tracking blood scent.

Master

In story after story, Father's dogs appear:
collies from the early years,

like Lassie, for the show I loved when little,
Dingle for an Irish isle his ancestors called home.

Mother remembers putting Lassie to sleep,
how us girls awakened to death's meaning.

Then came the Rottweilers, Bishop and Bridget,
with their block heads, slobber.

Father fed them under the table at dinner, remember—
we all rolled our eyes.

He didn't think we saw. Chad recalls
a hallway run-in, midnight bathroom trip,

when Bishop, Father's favorite, growled
but stayed. Chad breathed, walked past,

no blood was shed. From then on,
between them, détente.

Bishop lived to 12, nearly 93
in human years, an old soul.

One sister notes Bridget was with us
a while longer, a comfort, though no one can say

how she died. In the silence
before we call memory to us,

we see ourselves in the dark
with the animal of grief.

Self Portrait as Royal Palm

Roystonea regia, commonly known as the royal palm tree, is native to Florida and is used commonly in large residential landscapes, as well as in parks and lining streets and driveways.

My pinnate fingers terrify the homeowner board,
along with my roots, which they claim

reach deep enough to threaten a foundation.
Others can address my penetration,

but I hold firm in the climates and the altitudes,
refuge to the rare bonneted bat.

I impede some views, it's true, but the association
knew, or should have known, my nature

when landscapers placed me in the holes they dug
to help me settle, every snowbird's paradise incarnate,

yet how could I know I'd grow past
their expectations to sweep windows,

thrum my fan blades violently at times
across a labyrinth of panes, although I kissed them, too,

when the winds that blew across our wide Atlantic
paused to take a breath.

To Bartram, I was *Palma elata, Oreodoxa regia*
to Kunth. I understand I'm conspecific

with the Cuban version of myself.
My fruit was staple for the indigenous,

my ashen trunk used for canoes. Crown aside, above all,
to survive, I strive to reach for creature,

for that heart beside my own bud heart,
from which all new leaves come.

I Revisit My Father's Rooms in Anchorage

including the living, a solarium, the dining,
absent a table. The shower remodeled for easier access
had a window overlooking bushes thick

with raspberries my sister and I picked,
ate right there in the yard soon after the breakup,
found nothing like sweet Florida's.

I freeze-frame the glacial way he'd rise
from his recliner, brace against his walker to greet me—
when, in his day, he'd crave a ticket anyplace

adventure called—cathedrals, streets of cobblestone
in Florence, in Munich, whole itineraries
to trouble the ground his ancestors walked

imagine their ingress, egress,
until the diabetes beat his body down.
When my nieces ask about their late

grandfather, I say it's a shame
they'll never know him healthy, always with a plan.
How he would say, *my name is John, what's yours,*

to any handyman. How when he taught,
you'd never see him in a shirt
without pen clipped to pocket,

or outside without a proper hat.
He only wanted Florida again,
just one last time, before he died.

I see him coming or going near the portico,
his overflowing bookcase, coats racked trench to rain.
Hear background chimes mark time.

Hear Father translate nostalgia
from Greek roots: *return home* and *pain.*

Breath

Breath

Take Mozart, born for kings
and variations, the reach and slide

of the 40th symphony.
Or Monet in London, cycling in

and out of weather,
measuring his days in light.

How a body depends.

How waves break with dawn,
draw white caps past the shoreline.

What follows fire,
the grinning death.

What comes after the sun, the moon.

I Consider a Chair for My Mother's Apartment in Assisted Living

In the home section of the discount store,
I imagine Mother's legs failing
beneath her in the tiny space we rented
when we moved her out of her house

of 45 years and into *the facility,*
where she might seek purchase
in the bathroom, or the dining hall—

anyplace to fall, and what we might provide
to cushion the blow of the move.

She might rise from sinuous springs,
feet barely touching the laminate,
or propped on the cushy ottoman
we thought might fill a gap

where inches matter, where each day
she'll wake to a cat clock, blinded window
where wildlife, they say, are seen.

We hope an aide might open the shades
so she might look outside—
maintenance promised a feeder,
one of those suction kinds—

and imagine her stolen voice
in the trilling finches, hummingbirds.

Nutritional Value

Someone has a feeding tube
removed while I'm eating my Cobb
at TGI Fridays, thinking green is good this time
of year, since last evening's leftover pot roast

will send me over my quota of red
meat, the vitamins of carrots and potatoes
diminished after hours of simmer.

To course-correct. To devour on one's own,
savor the human and animal
juices. It's never enough: our agency, this vessel
we're poured into, out of.

Never forget the bleeding
of flavors, the tenderness
of shoulder falling from bone.

Lionfish Hunter

To kill a lionfish in the Western Atlantic
is to save a snapper, grouper, someone's legitimate dinner.

Is to manage the species' insatiable appetite,
rare as sashimi. Is to mitigate an unfolding tragedy.

Is to right reef life's equilibrium.
Is to gut red-white striped bodies, hunger's fire,

venomous spines within fins. Is to thwart
the dark heart lurking where it doesn't belong.

Is to murder without limits on sex or season,
grin satisfaction with each conquest.

Is to do it for money. Is to brave
spike after toxic spike in the mohawk.

Is to take one for the team. Is to imagine yourself
apex predator, dismembering helpless prey.

Is to protect yourself from yourself.
Is to relish each bloodletting, ventricle to atria.

Is to hope that just once, the consummation of your desire
could be permanent, keep invasion at bay.

Would feed you over and over.

Miami Mise-en-Scène

(1960s)

Summers, we'd drive from Tallahassee for Grandmother S.
and Lamar, rocking in the Florida room with Jackie Gleason
and away we go! and the show would go on, go on, go on forever.

Grandmother S. might be baking a coconut cake she'd nibble
a sliver of when done, or saving herself the heel a loaf, cut
and buttered to toast in the oven for dinner, our places

at the drop-leaf table set with her wedding sterling.
Beneath the white-hot sun, we'd melt, hold fists full of grapefruit,
big as our heads. In the garage, Lamar might strike a lighter, bent

for a smoke amidst a montage of tables and tools
we would never return to. He goes first, uprooted,
any spark long gone. I take Grandmother S. to senior day care,

a playpen of innocents in a room dubbed *activity*
where children become parents, grandparents become children,
like widows and orphans, broken figures in family paragraphs

unreconcilable in the body text, as if we tried but can't recall
where the story should go, where hands press over laps, *hello, hello,*
and I translate, *do I know you?*

My Father Hears Per Amore in His Apartment in Independent Living

He goes down for a nap—

dreams all the forgotten landmarks,
milestones, gaps in memory more than a home

once, twice removed, or a shared
history he can't see reflected
in his wife's eyes, a daughter's face,

a story we all once inhabited, erased.

Strains of Bocelli waft through the walls
as a guest emerges from a doorway

into a carpeted hall, a corridor of identical flats
separated by brass name plates. The music
of someone's final hours plays

out. Now and then he remembers
that summer vacation when the tortoise

crossed the island road and he stopped
the station wagon to capture it—
how attached we grew to the old gopher.

We see him now among the motes:
look how he dances, lands
like a light ray, or a song's high notes.

We are all our dust, Father says.

The Heart Contracts

Max leans his jaw forward into my hand
from the folded-down back seat
of the SUV, watches the country drive,
the trees race by. From his perspective
someone else is in control.

Minutes later his head falls
on the plain, white sheet.
It will happen to us all, eventually,
I know. He is old, but it's not time, it's just
not time, and just not just.

Returning him to the veterinarian,
I anticipate the follow-up: Improvement
since the pills? Next steps? How long until we see
a change with certainty, his rhythms stabilized?
Are we moving fast enough
from Point A to Point B?

Honey, won't you help me move the kennel,
he travels better in it,
I told my husband in advance. Push, heave.
Nothing arrives at its logical conclusion.

Now and then, bright eyes in the rearview
hint at reprieve: in a few days, he'll return
to chasing crows, I tell myself,
and with this hope, I let him go

wherever life may lead,
squeeze myself tight
in the space between bided time
and eternity, where our hearts both beat.
In between our breaths,
I believe.

Before Landfall

In the latest projection, Irma grazes
the spine of Florida's supine peninsula.

We track her path northwest on a weather app
from our safe room, where we lie on sleeping bags,

believe protection looks like this: doors, windows
shut tight, radio, flashlight, disaster plans at hand.

Minutes away, the winds off Cedar Key move inland.
First rainbands deluge our roof.

***

As the fluids left Father's body,
I watched him track my tears, a salt river

smelling of seaweed and grief.
His good eye would see me through

just one more storm, the mopping up I'd do,
so sure we'd not be swamped again.

***

Once again, we wait for havoc:
toppling oaks, transformer arcs,

for the house to tremble
as a freight train sound roars through,

as if to make up for lost time,
as if anticipation makes us safe.

***

When I was as tiny as a country
seen from light years away, Father held me

high above the swirling sea, that was
the beginning and the end of everything.

Ice-out

In the season built into Alaskans' DNA, when frozen rivers break apart and flow, mourners for Father alight like returning robins in the parking lot. Some shed studded tires, brave roadways flooded by snowmelt. On the stoop, like lingering starlings, guests peck necks and faces, others sidle inside. In the fellowship hall, the coffee pot the mourned manned singlehandedly for a decade percolates as if nothing has changed. The grief committee dresses dining tables in white, then separates each round, like ice cakes or floes breaking away. The room feels adrift. Soon, no one will taste the homemade dishes. In the chapel devoid of an organ and pews, someone rehearses a hymn at the lone piano. Perched in the rows of folding chairs, every two must share a hymnal, as a violinist bows a soothing tune. An elder from the men's group and a woman fresh from seminary will address the lost pastor's personhood. Select scripture will be shared. Congregants will relay the beloved's fondness for coffee cakes, his appearances at youth recitals and plays. His daughters will read Jane Kenyon poems, quote from Schweitzer and Tillich. One will stand on tiptoe in black dress pumps to reach the microphone until it amplifies her strain and she lets go to speak in her own small voice. Amazingly, it will carry, like a bird calling across the water.

Another Day's Breath

Another Day's Breath

What comes after the sun, the wren
that suddenly makes its night home
in the air plant. What flowers
throwing off seeds, then decays.

What spirit comes into your right heart
as mere blood, then pumps its way out,
stops, if you listen,

then starts again. What spirit knows
just how far back, how deep to go,
hugs your throat, kisses your lips
goodbye, hello.

My First House in Gainesville

where Max, a puppy, chewed my espadrilles,
gnawed the legs of the antique poplar cabinet
bought for a song in Tallahassee

years before my move. Where I settled
into the two-bedroom, split-plan ranch
with cornflower blue wallpaper

I soon applied, along with beige
transition tile and a kitchen backsplash,
making the space mine. When Mother came

to visit, we ate at the walnut drop-leaf table
I inherited from Grandmother S.—
cloth napkins on hand-woven mats

in her honor, proud to celebrate
what I finally owned. It's June again,
and new graduates pack local diners,

tube the Ichetucknee, where we drove
that white-hot day to float
in the cold spring. She kept a postcard

I found with her things. Now she's gone
and that home isn't mine. I puzzle the remnants
in my new rooms.

Ars Poetica: The Forms Themselves

Did I tell you the Galapagos Islands were something else—
their tumuli, domes, first life removed,
rethrown in thrust after volcanic thrust.
The guide shouted *lava* everywhere, and *pahoehoe,*
explained where it fell in the scheme of things,

and how the forms themselves could tell this story,
if only we would listen. Picture a wasteland—
fossilized soils, coral fragments
locked in stone. Flamingos fish from lagoons
in shadows of surrounding black,
out of the blue. Back when
and just then, I swear, they glowed.

The Felt Box

It comes down, the clerk says,
from across a felt box
full of shimmering pendants,

to whether I am a symmetrical
or an asymmetrical person,
to which synthetic—fake—

Australian opal would flatter me best,
regardless of shape or level
of fire. About how it feels to me

personally. Considering the options, I decide
there really is no question—

I will always choose a form
of safe attraction, nothing too off
center or flashy to square me away—

no question that exploding blues and purples
deeper than illusion, draws me
to this point, ready to pay

the 14-carat consequences,
letting a stranger weigh the gold
to offer me best price on two

simulated stones I favored, one
meandering fantasy, silhouette
of an island, the other, round

and too perfect, familiar
and just for that short time,
even knowing what I know,

I hang in that balance.

Blind Spots
(1990s)

for M. L.

We spin Mother's lazy Susan,
bowls of roasted chicken, green beans,

rimming the cedar round. We dish:
whoever might have died, my job,

European vacation. Max, my new pup,
the harness not holding him back.

Mother laughs, breaks in:
Labs, she says. *What do you want?*

How to begin: hunger, inherited
longing. My need to share my life,

be led. See the world
through an animal's eyes.

You and Mother nod.
You mention the tabby we'd had

as children. That terrible day, its cries.
I remember you looking up at me,

big sister. I went outside
to find the cat in agony,

Mother having backed right over it in the Skylark.
Stay in the house, I'd said,

but you ignored me,
and the tabby died its horrible death

and dies again as we relive
our first glimpse of the unseen.

We help ourselves to seconds,
pass the salt. I pray a little thank you

for not hating me, the sister
who couldn't shield you.

In turn, you thank me for trying.

The Day After Katie Died

is already afternoon. I show up on time
for my color and cut, because I'm a keeper
even on three hours of sleep.
My stylist makes small talk,
so I tell her part of me has died—

my animal, the part that listens
in the dark for heaves, hears every
tortured cry. Some count sheep, but I comb
for clues I might have missed, or flipped
to keep my hopes from dying.

The stylist razors my layers
as I tell her how our old dog, Katie, collapsed
on the kitchen tile—

Who knew dogs could scream, I say,
then how we scooped and toweled
her through the front door to the car

to the vet, and knew immediately
something was broken, irreparably.
How later, beckoned to *the quiet room*,
we saw our Katie for the last time
lying on a blanket—oh, her lifted head—

how she must have wondered why
she couldn't rise to greet us.
We could read her eyes.

Inside the hair apothecary, balms
for every texture and finish, spritz sprays
lined on shelves, along with creams

to quell self-doubt, the stylist blows
my nape hairs dry, my even ends.
Brushes me ever so gently out.

I blink to face my reframed face.

Seasonal Affective

Father's voice booms in on the second ring,
as if he never stopped speaking,

as if his words had never wavered,
or slurred. *He's fine*, we say, and return

to dismantling wreaths, stowing
another holiday season's bling,

habituated to shorter, darker days.
We keep reasons to hope on display.

When he falls again, before winter ends,
and EMTs reset him in his wheelchair,

weren't we past this, we ask, shake our heads *no*,
stuck in a fluctuating tempo.

When the chill penetrates our bones,
we pack our bags, meet spring on a beach,

where we let the waves
touch us gently, then recede.

My Father's German Words Come to Me

After the dog meanders his usual circle,
lifts a leg, completes his business, after coffee
—*mein Tagesablauf*, my father would say, *my routine*—

the sun rises, more stable than I'll ever be,
already burning. Once, he owned
a thousand books to check his meanings,

lost himself in any loose translation.
What's left of his library lives in a locked
storage locker I dream of opening,

only to close like the last great novel
I finished, sad that the journey of words—
story arc, final chapter, was over.

Abditive

—in memory of Debby Sundstrom

Like you, I have searched for best places to hide
where the lost might meander,
I'm once again young, who I am is a game

of come find me, surprise. I've sought to escape
what I once knew of bearings, honed

my own, pointed home, gone awry.

After natural disasters, the sheriffs would call
and you'd move house to house,
found a woman once, barely alive, by a tree,

commanded your dog, a warm body, to drop,
then draped her with your coat. You never

took credit. Years later, you followed the logic of footprints
to locate young Blake, scared and scratched
but unhurt, nudged under a bush

by his Rottweiler, Sam, who'd stayed with him
and growled on approach, but you coaxed

to your side with beef jerky. Despite lows in the 30s,
he wasn't cold, the boy said, then ate
the proffered oatmeal cookie.

The news reported Sam devoured a T-bone steak.

In hunting, you followed the Dao—spoke *dog*
others said, trailing off at the lack of apt words

to interpret abditives and fate.
I imagine wet kisses, reward

if I wait, if I'm patient, or go back in time
when I'm hidden in burrows, crevasses, my head,
greeted eigengrau dazed in dark space

seeking rescue, but mostly myself.
Now and then I confess I've been saved.

I Revisit What Comes to Me

My Father's German Words Come to Me Again

His story arc is over. I skirt my karst terrain
in Florida, mindful of sinking.

I say I'm blessed some mysteries still live
on my shelves unfinished, or unfathomed in the ecosystem.

What you don't know can't hurt you,
said Father, who knew everything.

In North Carolina, death was the outcome
he saw coming. Died in March before the time changed

and we turned clocks forward, our ears back,
for any echo we might interpret

as his voice. I was *das Kind*, the child
he kept my language from when plotting

an itinerary I wasn't allowed
to follow. Maybe the subject was boys

or curfews, or the contents of my diary
a sister had viewed. I never knew.

It's summer again and we dread new records,
stay inside. In the shadowed rooms,

Father's story opens like a tome,
like limestone I might plunge through,

into a sinkhole's glistening record
of earth's fossils, ocean, bone,

from which a name dislodges
I forgot I knew:

Mutti, bookmarked in memory's tongue.

My Sisters and I Tell the Children We Can't Have to Build a Castle

as if wet sand could teach
a youth's hands patience, or how to love

form's impermanence. We say,
feel your way, aim for consistency—

just-right viscosity to pack your walls,
make structures stick, stay steady.

We give them tools. We show them how:
plastic buckets, shovels. Molds,

a little hope. *Fight what might slip*
through your fingers. Dig a moat.

Did you know the human body
is composed of 60% water, I might ask,

let decomposition linger, unaddressed.
Let them be to carve their shapes.

When the sun sets and we head home
to shower, change, our unborn children stay

to mark the spot of their creation,
leave behind a labyrinth of towers,

bulwark against the tide. My sisters and I
mourn daily now what was,

what could have been, what died.
There, there, we say, as if to keep loss at bay,

as if they'll only lose a season
when their dreams wash away.

We Gather in Florida to Celebrate My Father's Life

Outside our hallway, cross-hatched feathers,
a flutter away from the hotel window,
perched hunter of the forest understory,

a red-shouldered hawk's eyes
meet our own, a window into which

we can't quite see, yet make our way—
third floor to first—open to story
after story, while outside a single magnolia,

gold-leafed in sun, backlights the first bloom,
as spring rain greens the asphalt oasis.

We greet our blood, catch up. Cousins
lament cousins outlived, out of touch,
who moved, who stayed, despite the odors

of smoke or strangers—reconstruct
commitments made, unmade, pursued,

as time realigned our views.
I give up my ghosts, and everything I know
of human nature, which is nothing.

Father is salt and mineral, crushed bone.
We arrange to arrange to arrange.

Did you know, I told the gathered group,
flowers from each state he lived in flank the pulpit,
bloom today in all of them, in all of you:
dogwood, peony, forget-me-not.

A Southern Black Racer Plays Dead in the Dollarweed

A frozen curve ten feet away, black sheen
on an island of mowed St. Augustine

in a resort full of snowbirds
where someone might perceive a pipe, perhaps a piece

of bent siding, death or its disguise
another, a native species, a lark—a novel sighting, serpentine—

might grab a hoe for quick dispatch
but I'm reminded how we burrow, seek refuge

in whatever landscape feels like home
until awakening to threat, we flee

we fly. I sense that soon he'll race
to safety, don't disturb, but inch within a stride of him—

white chin, gray underbelly
buried in the dollarweed, then sidestep

one yard shy of his body onto asphalt,
a sea of out-of-state-plates.

Some might not see a snake displaced,
but I'm in awe of *Coluber constrictor priapus*—

know why he hides.
Know nothing harmless here abides.

Take This History

Tragedy struck great-uncle Marshall, his family
after the war, Mother said.

I parse Marshall's papers for clues,
page through his darkness.

Fell out a fourth-floor window while sleepwalking,
the death certificate said, his age a cell

marked 36. Mother said he drank,
though it was never discussed.

I, too, imbibed when younger. Imagine a ledge
I could have leapt or fallen from

but something pulled me back.
A tragedy, Mother said, and said again,

when Julia, a cousin, newlywed, bled out,
kicked in the gut by a horse

yet Mother has medicine in her voice,
recounting the losses she outlived,

lest I read too much into things.

Take this history with a grain of salt.
You are more than DNA,

Mother assuages, tries to shake me free.

My Husband and I Engage in Estate Planning

When you asked me where we were,
with our wills and my advance directive,

I told you someone will always crave
the lost embrace, the felt thing,

impossible to give away or hold.
Always some aspect of belonging

eludes capture: the blood pressure cuff
still beeping its battery warning,

the rare laugh, with its octave of wheezes.
I could have said our joint accounts

were loans, illusory security, hunger a gift,
that clings to its beneficiaries. Instead,

I wished you'd take on my longing,
like a chore left incomplete when a shift

ends, and a worker finally clocks out.
I gave all my want to you, and you returned it

with interest, a credit to society, a lot
in life. I'll leave you my best guess

of usefulness, the protocols and processes
that made my job my life, my life,

my love, my darling. No words
can cover everything I couldn't tell you,

though you can't know yet what you
might miss. Where are we, you ask?

I write on the waiting paper, *Surrogate,*
your name, then—*breathe for me.*

Personal Effects

We shattered the frozen lock
in minus-ten degrees

to inventory the life Father left,
when, finally well enough to travel,

with all he could fit in a suitcase,
he fled Alaska for North Carolina

in the lower forty-eight. We were there,
but not all there. Some of us were missing

a list to lean on—but listless at the end,
he assumed we would devise intent

in his stored things—
in *shivelight lances*, Hopkins might say,

as we beam a flashlight on dropped table leaves,
a file case full of sermons. I seek a shade

of green, a favorite lithograph, unprepared to covet
a stack of hats, a notepad with stick-figured dogs

leashed to their walkers, or the passport
that expired last year, absent a single stamp.

Hope springs eternal, he'd say.
I'll take it all, on faith.

He might have left us a simple will to keep going.
A sister reclaims a carved pill box, a gift.

Opens the hidden lid
to the void she'll soon fly home.

Bodysuit

Facing the future, first Christmas
as orphan, I opened the plastic bag full of clothes
we'd taken from her true home

and her borrowed one, the last she'd known,
and came across my mother's bodysuit,
flashback in burnout lace—

a shade like Cabernet, so *holiday*, around the time
we knew she'd not be coming back
and all we had to do was empty.

Poured myself into her silhouette—
smooth waist, firm tuck, imagined I conformed
with give to spare, but when I pulled the garment overhead,

then slithered into hollow sleeves,
the spandex stretched to hold me in
—I almost couldn't breathe—

while between the thickness of my thighs
the bottom snaps refused to reach,
but why would they, and why would I

think anything she'd leave behind might fit me now
in this room of her spilled residuals,
so I change back to whatever form

claret, oxblood first found me in,
conjure Aphrodite. Outside, above a low brick ledge,
a snake's twisted shed.

The Changed Landscape

After office colleagues leave,
having talked over your head,

I dust your frame, arm's length away,
notice the magnolia tree behind you

blossoming despite the chill,
your eyes smiling beneath a felt fedora,

facing me focusing my lens,
never knowing I'd find you again

in my room each day,
across our weathered years—

frozen in that moment,
or that I'd scan, digitize,

then encase your print in glass
to protect you from the elements.

When I learn the magnolia's
Chinese ancestors programmed it

to bloom in the cold, the scene
unfolds with a fresh perspective:

snow by blossom, sunshine, stomata,
Asia by way of Decatur, now by then,

breathing in the past
to breathe again.

Notes

The epigraph at the front of this collection is the final stanza of Robert Frost's poem, "Revelation," from *A Boy's Will*, published first by David Nutt in London (1913), then in the United States by Henry Holt and Co. (1915).

The poem, "Abditive," was written after the death of a longtime work colleague of mine, Debby Sundstrom, a biological scientist at the University of Florida College of Veterinary Medicine. Debby was an animal lover whose personal commitment and dedication to dog training and search-and-rescue efforts for many years of her life were well known and respected in North Central Florida and elsewhere.

Several of the poems in *Bloodstream* are centered in Florida and North Carolina, the only two states I have ever lived in. Others reference the state of Alaska, which became part of my life in my early 40s, after my father moved to Anchorage to work as a pastor for a small church following retirement from his academic career. He ended up living there for over a dozen years (one of my sisters, who married a lifelong Alaskan and had his first grandchildren, had something to do with this). For these reasons, I associate Alaska with adventure and awe, as well as with my father's reinvention of himself in his later years. But my memories of Alaska, and the poems that reference it, also invariably wrestle with the difficulty of distance and familial separation.

Acknowledgments

I'm grateful to the editors of the following publications in which these poems first appeared (sometimes in slightly altered form and occasionally with different titles), and to those who have recognized this work elsewhere.

Alaska Women Speak: "We Gather in Florida to Celebrate My Father's Life" and "Ice-out"
Anacapa Review: "The Rose Bush"
Arsenic Lobster: "Ars Poetica: The Forms Themselves"
Atticus Review: "Self Portrait as Longleaf Pine"
Bear Review: "Ars Poetica: Negative Capability"
Body: "Wyeth's Women" and "Another Day's Inventory"
Bogg: "The Heart Contracts"
Cider Press Review: "Abditive"
Cottonwood: "Grandmother's Will"
Florida Review: "Globus"
Frontier Poetry: "Consistency"
Glass: "What I Tell My Unborn Children When They Ask Where We Come From" and "Anchorage"
Gravel: "Self Portrait as Royal Palm"
Hogtown Creek Review: "The Felt Box"
Palette Poetry: "The Land, The Sea, The Air" and "Orienteering"
Poetry Motel: "A Rare Disease"
Potomac Review: "Personal Effects"
Prolog: "Delivery"
Radar Poetry: "Friesian Story"
Rattle: "Nutritional Value"
Rise Up Review: "Making Soda Focaccia the Day of the Muslim Ban"
Split Rock Review: "Bearings"
Saint Katherine Review: "I Revisit My Father's Rooms in Anchorage"
South Florida Poetry Journal: "Take This History"

Stirring: "Lionfish Hunter" and "A Southern Black Racer Plays Dead in the Dollarweed"
Sugar House Review: "One Day's Inventory"
SWWIM: "Before Landfall"
The Christian Century: "The Changed Landscape"
Tule Review: "Breath"
UCity Review: "Blind Spots," "The Body Inside My Body," "For an Artist Painting Loss," "In the Men's Department," "Master," "My Father's German Words Come to Me Again," and "What Max Couldn't Tell Me of Desire"
Unknowns: "Discovery"

***

Several of these poems, sometimes in different forms, appeared in my previous chapbooks *Accommodations* (2019, Concrete Wolf Press Chapbook Award), and *The Heart Contracts* (2016, Finishing Line Press). The poem, "In the Men's Department" was a finalist for the Academy of American Poets College Prize when I was a graduate student at Florida State University in the early '80s.

I am beyond grateful to poet and professor Dr. William Woolfitt for his vision and editorial assistance in crafting this book. Without his encouragement, *Bloodstream* would never have been conceived, much less brought to fruition. In the book's later stages, Ida Stewart provided key editorial suggestions, which not only improved the manuscript, but also prompted me to think more deeply about each poem as a vessel for articulating my key themes of ancestral and environmental inheritances, embodied selves, and memory as an anchorage to shifting states of awareness and being. The final work reflects much of her thoughtful feedback.

To Lisa Zimmerman, Sean Sexton and Sally Rosen Kindred, the amazing poets who so generously made time to read and provide their insights into *Bloodstream*: please know how much I treasure the gift of your words. I am consistently amazed and moved by the support I have received for this work and my other poetry endeavors from friends and neighbors, colleagues, and members of the broad community of poets and writers I have encountered online and in-person; to be even a small part of such a rich fabric of writers working to bring their art into the world is an honor and a privilege. My sisters, my husband Chad, and so many of my friends have cheered me on throughout my journey. The blood of my late parents, along with all my ancestors and my lost beloved dogs, pulses within me, and always will.

I would also like to offer special thanks to my friend in poetry, Marissa Glover, who helped make the magic that would lead me to Mercer University Press.

No words can adequately express my deep gratitude to Marc Jolley, director of Mercer University Press, whose support brought this project to fruition. I will forever be grateful to him and to the MUP team for believing in me, and for their efforts in shepherding *Bloodstream* on its path from contract to publication.